THE
PASSIONATE
LIFE

BIBLE STUDY SERIES

TO THE
LOVERS
OF GOD

12-WEEK STUDY GUIDE

BroadStreet
PUBLISHING

D1416676

BroadStreet Publishing Group, LLC
Racine, Wisconsin, USA
BroadStreetPublishing.com

The Passionate Life Bible Study Series
LUKE: TO THE LOVERS OF GOD

© 2016 BroadStreet Publishing Group

Edited by Jeremy Bouma

ISBN-13: 978-1-4245-4994-8 (softcover)
ISBN-13: 978-1-4245-5251-6 (e-book)

Cover design by Chris Garborg at www.garborgdesign.com
Typesetting by Katherine Lloyd at www.theDESKonline.com

Printed in the United States of America
16 17 18 19 20 5 4 3 2 1

Contents

Using This Passionate Life Bible Study

The psalmist declares, "Truth's shining light guides me in my choices and decisions; the revelation of your Word makes my pathway clear" (Psalm 119:105).

This verse forms the foundation of the Passionate Life Bible Study series. Not only do we want to kindle within you a deep, burning passion for God and his Word, but we also want to let the Word's light blaze a bright path before you to help you make truth-filled choices and decisions, while encountering the heart of God along the way.

God longs to have his Word expressed in a way that would unlock the passion of his heart. Inspired by The Passion Translation but usable with any Bible translation, this is a heart-level Bible study, from the passion of God's heart to the passion of your heart. Our goal is to trigger inside you an overwhelming response to the truth of the Bible.

DISCOVER. EXPLORE. EXPERIENCE. SHARE.

Each of the following lessons is divided into four sections: *Discover the Heart of God; Explore the Heart of God; Experience the Heart of God;* and *Share the Heart of God.* They are meant to guide your study of the truth of God's Word, while drawing you closer and deeper into his passionate heart for you and your world.

The *Discover* section is designed to help you make observations about the reading. Every lesson opens with the same three questions: What did you notice, perhaps for the first time? What questions do you have? And, what did you learn about the heart of God? There are no right answers here! They are meant to jump-start your journey into God's truth by bringing to the surface your initial impressions about the passage. The other questions help draw your attention to specific points the author wrote and discover the truths God is conveying.

Explore takes you deeper into God's Word by inviting you to think more critically and explain what the passage is saying. Often there is some extra information to highlight and clarify certain aspects of the passage, while inviting you to make connections. Don't worry if the answers aren't immediately apparent. Sometimes you may need to dig a little deeper or take a little more time to think. You'll be grateful you did, because you will have tapped into God's revelation-light in greater measure!

Experience is meant to help you do just that: experience God's heart for you personally. It will help you live out God's Word by applying it to your unique life situation. Each question in this section is designed to bring the Bible into your world in fresh, exciting, and relevant ways. At the end of this section, you will have a better idea of how to make choices and decisions that please God, while walking through life on clear paths bathed in the light of his revelation!

The final section is *Share*. God's Word isn't meant to be merely studied or memorized; it's meant to be shared with other people—both through living and telling. This section helps you understand how the reading relates to growing closer to others, to enriching your fellowship and relationship with your world. It also helps you listen to the stories of those around you, so you can bridge Jesus' story with their stories.

SUGGESTIONS FOR INDIVIDUAL STUDY

Reading and studying the Bible is an exciting journey! It's like reading your favorite novel—where the purpose is encountering the heart and mind of the author through its characters and conflict, plot points, and prose.

This study is designed to help you encounter the heart of God and let his Word to you reach deep down into your very soul—all so you can live and enjoy the life he intends for you. And like with any journey, a number of practices will help you along the way:

1. Begin your lesson time in prayer, asking God to open up his Word to you in new ways, show areas of your heart that need teaching and healing, and correct any area in which you're living contrary to his desires for your life.

2. Read the opening section to gain an understanding of the major themes of the reading and ideas for each lesson.

3. Read through the Scripture passage once, underlining or noting in your Bible anything that stands out to you. Reread the passage again, keeping in mind these three questions: What did you notice, perhaps for the first time? What questions do you have? What did you learn about the heart of God?

4. Write your answers to the questions in this Bible study guide or another notebook. If you do get stuck, first ask God to reveal his Word to you and guide you in his truth. And then, either wait until your small group time or ask your pastor or another respected leader for help.

5. Use the end of the lesson to focus your time of prayer, thanking and praising God for the truth of his Word, for what he has revealed to you, and for how he has impacted your daily life.

SUGGESTIONS FOR SMALL GROUP STUDY

The goal of this study is to understand God's Word for you and your community in greater measure, while encountering his heart along the way. A number of practices will also help your group as you journey together:

1. Group studies usually go better when everyone is prepared to participate. The best way to prepare is to come having read the lesson's Scripture reading beforehand. Following the suggestions in each individual study will enrich your time as a community as well.

2. Before you begin the study, your group should nominate a leader to guide the discussion. While this person should work through the questions beforehand, his or her main job isn't to lecture, but to help move the conversation along by asking the lesson questions and facilitating the discussion.

3. This study is meant to be a community affair where everyone shares. Be sure to listen well, contribute where you feel led, and try not to dominate the conversation.

4. The number one rule for community interaction is: nothing is off-limits! No question is too dumb; no answer is out of bounds. While many questions in this study have "right" answers, most are designed to push you and your friends to explore the passage more deeply and understand what it means for daily living.

5. Finally, be ready for God to reveal himself through the passage being discussed and through the discussion that arises out of the group he's put together. Pray that he would reveal his heart and revelation-light to you all in deeper ways. And be open to being challenged, corrected, and changed.

Again, we pray and trust that this Bible study will kindle in you a burning, passionate desire for God and his heart, while impacting your life for years to come. May it open wide the storehouse of heaven's revelation-light. May it reveal new and greater insights into the mysteries of God and the kingdom-realm life he has for you. And may you encounter the heart of God in more fresh and relevant ways than you ever thought possible!

Introduction to the Gospel of Luke

With the analytical precision of a doctor, Luke investigates with first-hand knowledge those who had seen what Jesus did and heard what Jesus taught. He gives us a full picture of Jesus' life and ministry, applying scrupulous accuracy to all he wrote to ensure that what we read is factual.

Luke takes his readers through Jesus' entire ministry career to reveal how Jesus is the true hope of the world. He also shows how God has been faithful to Israel and the promises he gave her. He invites the nations to the table of Christ's love and hope. It is a book for everyone, for we all need mercy. Luke writes clearly of the humanity of Jesus—as the servant of all and the sacrifice for all. Every barrier is broken down in Luke's gospel: between Jew and Gentile, men and women, rich and poor. In Luke, we see Jesus as the Savior of all who come to him.

We've designed this study to help you discover the mercy of God through Luke's detailed, historical analysis of history's most fascinating person, Jesus of Nazareth. Each lesson is divided into four sections: the "Discover" section is designed to help you make observations about the reading; section 2, "Explore," takes you deeper into God's Word by inviting you to think more critically and explain what the passage is saying; "Experience" questions are designed to help you apply the heart of God to your own life; and the final section will help you share God's life and heart with others.

This world is a far better place because of the "autopsy" Dr. Luke performs in his gospel on Jesus' life, death, and resurrection. We hope you discover what Luke unveils: Jesus is the One you've been waiting for your whole life!

Lesson 1

The Story of Promised Hope

LUKE 1:1–2:52

"Glory to God in the highest realms of heaven! For there is peace and a good hope given to the sons of men." (Luke 2:14)

Today's passage contains powerful encouragement and hope for future blessing, especially for those who long and dream for a child.

It begins with Zechariah, the husband of elderly, barren Elizabeth. One day while Zechariah was on the job, something unusual happened. An angel brought him startling yet hopeful news: their prayers for a child were being answered! Not long after, their hopelessness was turned upside down, for they expected a child.

Then there was Miriam,[1] so young and so full of hope. And engaged! But in the midst of her hope and excitement as a bride-to-be, she also met uncertainty. Like Zechariah, an angel visited Miriam with a message: she was going to have a baby. But how, since she was still a virgin? The angel reassured her with words that will resonate with hope in every heart: "Not one promise from God is empty of power, for with God there is no such thing as impossibility!" (1:37). These words are for all people, too, because the baby she birthed was the promised hope of the world!

---

1 "Miriam" is a literal rendering from the original Greek and Aramaic, which leave the Hebrew as is. She is more widely known as Mary, mother of Jesus.

Discover the Heart of God

- After reading Luke 1:1–2:52, what did you notice, perhaps for the first time? What questions do you have? What did you learn about the heart of God?

- Why did Luke say he wrote his Gospel, and how did he write it?

- Who were Zechariah and Elizabeth? What happened to them individually, and how did they react? Compare their reactions.

- How did Miriam respond to the angel's news? What did the angel say in response, and what did he say about the soon-to-be-born baby Jesus?

- When Miriam and Joseph left Jerusalem after a Passover trip, they discovered twelve-year-old Jesus was missing! Where was he, what was he doing, and why did it make sense?

Explore the Heart of God

- According to the Gospel of Luke, why can we be confident in Luke's account of Jesus' story?

- Zechariah was visited by an angel and told he would have a son, later named John. How was John's birth a fulfillment of Old Testament prophecies concerning the Messiah?

- Understandably, Miriam was shocked at the idea of being pregnant, because she was a virgin! Why does it matter to Jesus' identity and our salvation that he was "born of a virgin," as the ancient Christian creeds affirm?

- In response to the amazing news that she was going to bear and birth the Son of God, Miriam burst into a prophetic song to the Lord. How is what she said connected to Israel's own story and their anticipation of the Messiah?

- How did the events surrounding Jesus' birth specifically fulfill Old Testament prophecies? Can you identify some of these?

- In 2:26, God had made a promise to Simeon. We don't know exactly how long Simeon held on to this promise, but we do see he kept faith in God. More importantly, we see that God remained faithful. What does this show you about God? Why was he faithful to his promise? What does Simeon's song tell you about how significant it was to him to see Jesus?

Experience the Heart of God

- In this reading, a number of people experience the heart of God through promises. What promises have you received from God and seen fulfilled?

- Consider the story of Zechariah. God was faithful to his prayers even when he stopped praying them. What prayers have you prayed for in the past, but like Zechariah have given up praying? What does it mean to you that God remembered Zechariah's prayers long after he stopped praying them?

- Have you ever received shocking, bewildering news like Miriam? How did you experience the heart of God in the midst of that news?

- The angel armies proclaimed that "peace and a good hope" had been given to the world (2:14). How have you experienced this truth as you've experienced the heart of God?

- It seems clear that Simeon had been waiting his whole life for the appearing of The Refreshing of Israel. Yet he waited patiently and saw fulfillment. How should his example inspire our own experience with the heart of God and the promises he has breathed over our lives?

Share the Heart of God

- Miriam had her own plans for her life. While God's plan for her fulfilled those dreams, it was more than she could have asked or imagined! How can her example inspire others as you share the heart of God for them?

- There are some people in your life who've been waiting a long time for their dreams to find fulfillment, like Simeon. What might the Holy Spirit want to say to them as you share the heart of God using Simeon's story?

- Simeon prophesied that Jesus would be "the revelation light for all people everywhere!" (2:32). What does this truth mean for those in your life?

- Consider the example of the prophetess named Anna. How should her response at seeing Jesus guide our own response, especially when it comes to sharing the heart of God?

CONSIDER THIS

Our God is a promising God and a God who stays true to his promises of hope! His ultimate promise, stretching all the way back to the beginning of time, was the birth of a savior who would rescue us from evil, sin, and death. Thank God for fulfilling this promise in Jesus and all the promises he has made to you, which he is always faithful to fulfill.

Lesson 2

The Mighty One Has Arrived!

LUKE 3:1–4:30

*"There is one coming who is mightier than I.
He is supreme. In fact, I'm not worthy of even being
his slave ... he will baptize you into the Spirit of holiness
and into his raging fire."* (Luke 3:16)

What makes a great person great? What are the signs of a great leader? John the Immerser was a great person. As we saw in the section from Luke in the last lesson, John was commissioned by God as his prophet, a forerunner to pave the way for God's Anointed One and prepare people to embrace his ways. Eventually, the people thought John could be the Great One they had been waiting for, the Messiah. Yet there was one who was greater than even John: Jesus was the greatest person who ever lived; he was the Mighty One!

In today's reading, we discover how mighty Jesus really is. When he was baptized, a mighty voice from heaven declared his supreme identity. Then Jesus was tempted and tested in the wilderness by the Devil himself, yet he didn't give in. Instead, he resisted! Armed with the Holy Spirit's power, he launched a powerful, provocative teaching ministry, where he unveiled the majesty and presence of God's kingdom realm.

No doubt our world has great people, but Jesus is greater and mightier! He is the Mighty One who came to rescue us and give us God's good life.

Discover the Heart of God

- After reading Luke 3:1–4:30, what did you notice, perhaps for the first time? What questions do you have? What did you learn about the heart of God?

- What did John the Immerser do as part of his ministry? What was his message? How did it prepare people "to see the life of God" (4:6)?

- How did John respond when people wondered if he was the Messiah?

- What happened when Jesus came to John the Immerser to be baptized? What happened to Jesus afterward?

- After Jesus was tested, he was armed with the Holy Spirit and taught in synagogues. What did he teach in one setting when he read from Isaiah?

Explore the Heart of God

- John the Immerser brought a provocative message everywhere he went, warning people to repent. According to 3:3 and 3:8, what does it mean to repent?

- Who was the Messiah, and why were the people of Israel waiting for him?

- What rich theological concept and picture of God is revealed through Jesus' baptism? Why is what the heavenly voice spoke over Jesus so crucial to his identity?

- Jesus' genealogy in 3:23–38 shows how his human lineage through Miriam traces back to David and his throne. It also becomes a tour through God's historic promises, from Adam to Abraham to David, showing that one day he would send a savior. What does this reveal about the heart of God, that he would trace it throughout history?

- How did Jesus respond to the Devil's testing? What is a deeper revelation truth we should glean from this insight?

- Reread 4:16–20, which contains a quote from the book of Isaiah. How did Jesus fulfill these prophecies of Isaiah throughout his life?

Experience the Heart of God

- John's message was revolutionary, for the religion of the day taught that forgiveness could only be found temporarily by offering sacrifices in the temple. John had a different message: forgiveness of sin was a heart issue, not gained by religious ritual. Repentance is more important than religious acts. Why is this relevant today as much as in John's day to experiencing the heart of God?

- John the Immerser said every "tree" must "produce fruit." Consider your own life and its "fruit." Where do you see some areas that could grow and change so that you produce what John says God longs for from us?

- How have you experienced the truth of what Jesus said he came to do in 4:18–19?

Share the Heart of God

- Like John the Immerser, how can we prepare people "to see the life of God" (4:6)?

- Jesus went into the wilderness immediately after his Father declared love for him and the Holy Spirit came upon him. In such a short time, he went from perhaps the highest point of his life to what might have been the lowest before his crucifixion. What helped Jesus make it through his difficult testing, and how might this be an encouragement to others?

- What does Jesus' experience in his hometown remind us when it comes to sharing the heart of God with those we know?

CONSIDER THIS

There has never been as great or as mighty a person as Jesus! He is the Mighty One who came to do what we could not do for ourselves. He was anointed to be hope for the poor, freedom for the brokenhearted, healing for the sick, and release for those in bondage. He also bore a message of God's saving goodness, which is good news for all people! Consider how he has worked mightily on your behalf. Then spending time praising him for it.

Lesson 3

———

First Impressions

LUKE 4:31–6:49

"To prove to you all that I, the Son of Man,
have the lawful authority on earth to forgive sins,
I say to you now, stand up! Carry your stretcher
and go on home, for you are healed." (Luke 5:24)

No one made a first impression like Jesus! Yet it's clear that, from the very beginning, Jesus was received with mixed reviews. He was a sensation all right, but people didn't exactly know what to make of him. So they tried to fit him into their own little box; they tried to make him dance according to their tune.

Yet Jesus defied boxes. He was his own person, primarily because he came with his own message and to fulfill his own mission. From the start of his ministry, he made it clear who he was: Lord. Jesus is Lord over any of the accuser's temptations; over both Jews and Gentiles; over sickness and any natural power; over any demonic power; over the Sabbath; and over our lives.

Jesus danced to no one's agenda but his Father's. And incredibly, within his lordship he showed us who God is and what he is like. He set captives free, opened the eyes of the blind, and lifted burdens from the oppressed. He manifested God's love to us and calls us to submit to his lordship by doing the same.

May Luke's impression of Jesus make an impression on you, drawing you closer to your Savior.

Discover the Heart of God

- After reading Luke 4:31–6:49, what did you notice, perhaps for the first time? What questions do you have? What did you learn about the heart of God?

- What happened when Jesus was teaching in a congregation in Galilee? How did Jesus respond to the interruption? (See 4:31–37)

- What was it that caused Jesus to forgive the sins of the paraplegic and then heal him? Why were the Pharisees angry about this?

- Who was Matthew, and what happened when he encountered Jesus? Why did the Pharisees later complain to Jesus' disciples about his encounter with Matthew and his friends?

- In Luke 6:20–26, we find two lists of two kinds of people: people who are "blessed" and those who are "sorrowful." List these two kinds of people, comparing what they experience.

- What did Jesus teach should be our response to enemies? What about judging others and our generosity toward others?

Explore the Heart of God

- What did Jesus mean when he said that Simon Peter's new calling was to "catch men for salvation"? What does this mean for our own calling in the world?

- In 5:12, a leper said to Jesus that if he was only willing to heal him, he could do so completely. What does it tell us about the heart of God that Jesus responded, "Of course I am willing to heal you," and did?

- What did Jesus mean by the question he asked the Pharisees in 5:31, when he overheard them complaining? How does it relate to Jesus' mission and God's heart?

- Luke emphasized Jesus' lordship in these chapters, but another focus is how blinded the religious leaders were by their rules. Jesus addressed this specifically in 5:27–32 and 6:1–11. What do you learn about God's heart through these passages?

- What does the reaction by the religious leaders to Jesus' healing reveal about their religious rules versus Jesus' compassion?

- What did Jesus mean that "trees" are revealed by the kind of fruit that they produce? What does this have to do with experiencing the heart of God?

Experience the Heart of God

- At every turn in Luke's Gospel, Jesus asserted his lordship to defeat the powers of darkness in people's lives. What areas of your life need his lordship to bring his light? How can you bring his light to someone you know who needs it?

- Where in your life are you tentatively asking if Jesus is "willing" to respond to your own needs? How should Jesus' response to the leper inspire confidence in your experience of the heart of God?

• Luke said Jesus ate with sinners and came to "call those who fail to measure up and bring them to repentance" (5:32). Why is this good news for you and your own experience of the heart of God?

• Jesus made it clear we have a choice. Having heard his words, we can either follow them or ignore them. His sermon gives us wisdom for bearing good fruit and having a successful life. Did God highlight part of Jesus' sermon for you? Ask him how you can grow in Jesus' wisdom for your life.

• Luke 4:32 says Jesus "stunned and dazed" the people with his teachings. When was a time you experienced a similar stunning and dazing at something Jesus taught you about the heart of God?

Share the Heart of God

- Jesus said that the era of God's "great acceptance" had dawned. Do you feel the truth that you are accepted by God? If not, then receive this truth today. If yes, then how can you share God's acceptance with others?

- What does it say about the people who met Jesus early in his ministry that they "held him tightly" and didn't want him to go? What does this mean for sharing him and God's heart with people in your life?

- Explain the role miracles and good works played in spreading the news about Jesus and how they might help in sharing the heart of God.

- What does it reveal about God's heart that Jesus ate with those at the bottom of society? How should this impact how you share God's heart?

- Do you have an enemy, or have you experienced persecution and trouble at the hands of others? How might it look to share the heart of God by following Jesus' teachings on loving your enemies?

CONSIDER THIS

Jesus makes two things clear: First, everything will submit to his lordship, yet we can choose to submit willingly today. Second, those who submit to his lordship are healed, saved, and set free. Commit yourself for the first time or renew your commitment to Jesus' lordship over your life today.

Lesson 4

Jesus, Are You the One?

LUKE 7:1–8:21

"Are you the coming Messiah we've been expecting, or are we to continue to look for someone else?" (Luke 7:20)

There's a God-shaped hole in all of us, a void that we're waiting to be filled. Some people search for that fulfillment through a number of ways, whether through relationships, money, meaning and purpose, or substances. Others never seem to find what they've been waiting for.

In the middle of today's reading, we find someone who'd been waiting for God to show up in his life and his people's lives for some time: John the Immerser. He thought Jesus might be the one they'd been waiting for to rescue them. So he sent some people to ask him.

How did Jesus answer them? "Take a look at what I've been doing!" The evidence was so overwhelming, the truth could not be denied that Jesus was the One that John and all of Israel—all the *world*—had been waiting for! Not when everyone who came to him was healed, set free, made whole, and given hope.

In this passage, you'll meet others who experienced the truth of this coming through tangible ways too. And Jesus taught a spiritual story to illustrate how we should respond to his coming and his message.

Jesus is the One you've been waiting for your whole life. Believe it and experience it!

Discover the Heart of God

- After reading Luke 7:1–8:21, what did you notice, perhaps for the first time? What questions do you have? What did you learn about the heart of God?

- What did the two disciples of John the Immerser ask Jesus? What was his response?

- One evening Jesus was invited to dine with a Jewish religious leader, Simon. What happened during the dinner, and how did Simon respond? How did Jesus?

- While on a ministry tour through the countryside, Jesus told a spiritual story about a farmer who sowed seed. Describe the story in your own words.

- Why did Jesus say we need to pay close attention to our hearts?

Explore the Heart of God

- Why did Jesus have such good words to say about the Roman captain? What did the captain do that led Jesus to heal his servant?

- When disciples of John the Immerser asked Jesus if he was the one they were waiting for, he answered them in an interesting way. How does Jesus' answer connect to what they're asking?

- Jesus contrasted his behavior with John's behavior in 7:33–35. He ended his comparison by pointing to neither John nor himself, but to wisdom. What do you think Jesus meant that God's wisdom would be "proven true by the expressions of godliness in everyone who follows me" (7:35)?

- In response to Simon's disapproval of the immoral woman, Jesus told a story. What point was Jesus trying to make to Simon?

- What did Jesus mean by his spiritual story about the four kinds of seeds? Why does this story reveal so much about the mysteries of God's kingdom realm?

Experience the Heart of God

- What can Jesus' response to the grieving mother who lost her son reveal to us about our own experience of God's heart in our times of grief?

- In essence, Jesus told John's disciples to see what he was doing as proof that he was who he said he was and what they'd been waiting for. How have you experienced the truth of Jesus in your own life?

- Jesus said in 7:28 that John the Immerser was the greatest man up to that point in history—greater than King David, Noah, Abraham, Elijah, or Daniel! But his promise was that anyone in his kingdom is even greater than John. What does this truth mean in your life?

- Read what Jesus said about the woman in 7:44–47. How can you welcome Jesus into your life as this woman did?

- Consider your own response to the heart of God in relation to Jesus' spiritual story about the four seeds. How have you responded? What seed are you?

Share the Heart of God

- People have been waiting for Jesus their whole lives, whether they know it or not. Like John and his disciples, how can you show and share the truth of this with those in your life?

- Jesus said the immoral woman's sins were forgiven and her faith in Jesus had given her life. Why is that such good news to those in your life who need to experience the heart of God?

CONSIDER THIS

Jesus is the One you've been waiting for your whole life! He proved who he was by the signs he performed to transform people's lives. Our transformed lives are signs that point to him today. If you have believed in Jesus but have not yet seen him transform your life, come to him in faith today and let the transformation begin.

Lesson 5

The Signs of the Mighty One

LUKE 8:22–9:62

*"Who is this man who has authority over winds
and waves that they obey him?"* (Luke 8:25)

What do a storm, a demon-possessed man, a bleeding woman, a young daughter, and baskets of food have in common? They're all signs of the Mighty One, the Messiah, Jesus Christ!

These five miracles are a small handful of signs that represent Jesus' might. There's one other thing these events also have in common. Faith. In each of these episodes, people either had or lacked faith in Jesus. On both the sea and the hillside with the crowd, the disciples lacked faith in Jesus, yet he worked to save them and feed the people anyway. Both the Jewish leader and the bleeding woman had faith, which Jesus said released their healing. Even the demons that possessed the man knew who Jesus was, his power and might, and they trembled!

When we sit with the signs of the Mighty One, we can't help but ask the question the disciples asked: Who is this man? Who indeed! He is the Mighty One, the Anointed One—God's Messiah. And his mighty miracles are signs that point to this truth.

Discover the Heart of God

- After reading Luke 8:22–9:50, what did you notice, perhaps for the first time? What questions do you have? What did you learn about the heart of God?

- When Jesus returned to Galilee, two people needed his help. Who were they, what did they need, and what common element solved their problem?

- One day when Jesus was teaching the crowds, the disciples were concerned about feeding the people. How did Jesus respond and what did he do?

- When Jesus asked his disciples, "Who do people think I am?" what did they say? Then how did they respond to his second question: "But who do you believe that I am?"

- While Jesus and three disciples were on the mountain, a man below brought his sick son to the remaining disciples for healing, yet they couldn't heal the boy. Why not?

Explore the Heart of God

- When the disciples crossed the lake of Galilee, a fierce storm threatened their boat. It was so bad they thought they were going to drown! Jesus asked them why they were so fearful and why they had lost their faith in him. How was their fear a sign that they lacked faith in Jesus?

- So far in Luke's Gospel, faith in Jesus has been a common element in Jesus healing, forgiving, and releasing people. What do we learn about faith in these examples, especially in 8:40–56?

• Why do you suppose the townspeople became frightened at Jesus' amazing power? What does this tell us about some people's reactions to the heart of God in Christ?

• What is the significance of what Jesus did with his disciples in 9:1–2, especially in light of the previous five chapters?

• What does the passage about Jesus' true glory in 9:28–36 reveal about the Father's heart toward Jesus?

• Our reading ends with Jesus inviting several people to follow him, yet they give some interesting responses. How should their excuses and Jesus' responses inform how we ourselves respond to Jesus' invitation to experience the heart of God by following him?

Experience the Heart of God

- Because of Jesus, a mad man was totally set free from his demon. His release was so complete that he was "clothed, speaking intelligently, and sitting at the feet of Jesus" (8:35). How have you yourself experienced Jesus and his power in these ways?

- Both Jairus and the bleeding woman brought their needs to Jesus in faith, trusting he had the power and desire to help. Spend some time bringing your own needs to Jesus in faith, trusting what they trusted.

- When Jesus sent his disciples on mission, he told them to take nothing with them. Not a staff or backpack, not food or money—not even a change of clothes! What does this tell us about our own experience of God's heart for us and our mission on his behalf?

- "Who do you say I am?" is a question Jesus asks everyone. How would you respond?

- Jesus said in 9:55 that he didn't come to destroy life but to bring it to the world. What does this reveal about the heart of God, and how have you experienced this truth yourself?

Share the Heart of God

- It's remarkable that Jesus sent the healed man from Gerasenes on mission rather than taking him along on his. What did he tell him to do, and how should this inspire us to share the heart of God?

- Do you know anyone who has suffered physically, emotionally, or mentally for long periods of time? What encouragement could you give them from the story of the woman in 8:42–48?

- When Jesus sent the disciples to share the heart of God, he told them to remain in places that welcomed them and leave places that rejected them (9:45). How should this inform how we share God's heart too?

- When the disciples discovered someone not from their group casting out demons in Jesus' name, they told him to stop. Yet Jesus said it was okay. How might his response teach us to share the heart of God in partnership with others?

CONSIDER THIS

The same Anointed One who kept the disciples safe, freed a demon-possessed man, healed a daughter and woman, and fed thousands is ready, willing, and able to do the same for you and your life. Ask God to give you the faith the disciples lacked but that Jairus and the bleeding woman had, in order to experience what they themselves experienced.

Lesson 6

Love Is a Verb

LUKE 10:1–12:59

*"You must love the Lord God with all your heart,
all your passion, all your energy, and your
every thought. And you must love your neighbor
as well as you love yourself."* (Luke 10:27)

Jesus' teachings and life have the incredible ability to cut to the heart of the matter, revealing our heart and its true intentions, with all of its self-deception and self-justification. In a moment of crystal-clear clarity, Jesus exposed the heart of one man when the man tried to justify his own inaction by testing Jesus with a question: "Teacher, what requirement must I fulfill if I want to live forever in heaven?" (10:25).

Jesus confirmed the man was called to love God fully and love his neighbors as well as he loved himself. But the man pressed in, asking Jesus to define his "neighbor," revealing his true motives and heart. The man wanted Jesus to define the boundaries of his neighborly love. He wanted to know who—and more importantly, who *not*—to love, so he went in search of a loophole.

Jesus' answer, while it can test our hearts, truly revealed God's heart. Throughout this lesson he insists that love requires faithful action. Mercy, compassion, and justice aren't bumper-sticker philosophies. They must become part of who we are and what we do for a hurting world.

Discover the Heart of God

- After reading Luke 10:1–12:59, what did you notice, perhaps for the first time? What questions do you have? What did you learn about the heart of God?

- After Jesus formed teams of disciples, he released them with a set of instructions. What did he tell them? Then what did they report back when they returned? What did Jesus report?

- Why did Jesus frequently refer to "this generation" as "evil"? What was it about their posture to the heart of God that warranted such a description?

- In 12:4–5, Jesus told us to fear God, who has power over our soul. How did he follow up this warning in 12:6–7?

- Jesus described two kinds of managers in a spiritual story. Who were they, and what did Jesus say about them?

- How can we be prepared for our own Master's return? How do you think it looks to keep alert and ready for his return?

Explore the Heart of God

- What does it mean that God's kingdom realm has arrived and is within people's reach?

- It can be easy to become distracted like Martha instead of sitting at Jesus' feet like Miriam,[1] as we see in 10:38–42. What did Miriam gain and Martha lose by the choices they made?

- A religious scholar asked Jesus, "What do you mean by 'my neighbor'?" (10:29) and then Jesus told a story. How did this story answer the man's question? Who does Jesus end up saying is our neighbor?

- The prayer Jesus gave his disciples in 11:2–4 has what we could call six "stanzas." Explain them and how they are the perfect way to experience the heart of God.

1   "Miriam" is a literal rendering from the original Greek and Aramaic, which leave the Hebrew as is. She is more widely known as Mary, the sister of Martha.

- Jesus said in 12:33–34 to not worry about earthly treasures but about eternal ones. Then in 13:1–5 he used an earthly disaster to warn people of eternal disaster. What is Jesus saying to us in his continual emphasis?

- Jesus warned in 13:22–30 that many will seek to come into his kingdom but not find the way in. What do you see in these verses as the way to enter his kingdom?

Experience the Heart of God

- Would you say your experience of the heart of God is more like Martha's or Miriam's?

- Jesus told us to "ask ... seek ... and knock" when it comes to praying. What is one thing you can bring to the Lord in prayer, trusting that one day heaven's door will open for you?

- We have already seen Jesus send people on missions twice, instructing them to not worry about their provisions but to trust in God. In 12:22–34, he expanded this even more. How can you grow in your trust that God will always take care of you?

- The parables Jesus taught in 13:18–21 show that something small can still have great impact. This can encourage us deeply that any of us can impact the world deeply. What small thing can you do for God's kingdom today that can grow to have great impact?

Share the Heart of God

- Who do you know who's "ripe" for the harvest? How might the Owner of the Harvest want to drive you out into their lives? How can you share the heart of God with them through acts of neighborly love?

- It's no secret that many in our culture have been burned by the church, like others were burned by the Pharisees. How can we acknowledge and repent of what Jesus accused the Pharisees of doing in 11:39–52 as we share the heart of God?

- In what way could sharing the heart of God found in 12:22–32 encourage someone you know?

- In 13:10–17, Jesus sharply answered his critics because they had made their rules so important that they couldn't recognize love in action when they saw it. How can you put love in action and share God's heart with those in your life?

CONSIDER THIS

Jesus' life is shining proof that love is a verb; it takes action. Incredibly, he invites us to join him in this divine expression both by receiving his powerful love and by becoming his expression of love to those around us. Ask God today to meet you afresh with his love and show you how to give that love away to others in practical ways.

Lesson 7

———

The Way of the Kingdom

LUKE 13:1–15:31

"There are some who are despised and viewed as the least important now, but will one day be placed at the head of the line. And there are others who are viewed as elite today who will become least important then." (Luke 13:30)

Through both his teachings and his spiritual stories, Jesus taught us to live for the future eternity that awaits us. He traced several themes through his teachings, themes of future-minded living, faithfulness, and care for the needy. This last theme is particularly key because it frames the others.

Jesus clearly demonstrated this heart by healing those in need and by sending others to heal those in need. We hear this heart in his rebuke of those who refuse to have compassion on people. We understand it in his stories of how heaven rejoices when the lost is found. His point is most clear in his stories of those who comfort themselves in this life at the expense of those who have no comfort.

God cares for the needy. Why else would he send Jesus to die for us? And Jesus made it clear that we live for God when we love like him, joining him in compassion to genuinely care for those in need. This is how we build a life that is safeguarded from crashing down. This is the way of God's kingdom realm.

Discover the Heart of God

- After reading Luke 13:1–15:31, what did you notice, perhaps for the first time? What questions do you have? What did you learn about the heart of God?

- How did the experts of the law reply to Jesus' question about healing and what they would do if their animals fell into a well on the Sabbath?

- Jesus said in 14:7–14 that we should take the humble position whenever we can. What was his purpose behind saying this?

- In 14:25–33, Jesus outlined a number of "costs" of following him. List those costs.

• What was the response every time a lost item was found in Luke 15?

Explore the Heart of God

• Jesus taught that there was a great "cost" for those who "enter through the narrow doorway to God's kingdom realm" (13:24). What kind of cost did Jesus mean, and why is the doorway into the kingdom narrow?

• How are the smallest seeds planted and yeast like God's kingdom realm?

• What was God's intent for the Sabbath? Why was it made? Based on Jesus' question in 14:1–6, what had the Pharisees turned it into?

• What do you think was Jesus' message in his spiritual story about the man who invited many to join him in a great feast?

• In 14:33, we find one of Jesus' more challenging statements. Read it again and then explain what the heart of God is in this.

• Most people know 15:11–32 as the parable of the prodigal son, but it's really more about the Father's heart. What do you see about the heavenly Father's heart in this parable?

Experience the Heart of God

• Jesus said God's kingdom realm starts off tiny but experiences explosive growth and effect. How have you experienced this yourself? In what small ways can you help spread God's kingdom realm?

- In Jesus' story about the man who had a great feast in 14:16–24, everyone found excuses for why they couldn't come. How can you respond to Jesus today with no excuses?

- Which of the costs Jesus listed in 14:25–35 is the most difficult for you? How might he be asking you to count the costs to more fully follow him?

- How does it make you feel to know God is like a shepherd who has lost a sheep, a woman who has lost a coin, and a father who has lost his son? How does it deepen your experience of his heart?

• The song "Amazing Grace" captures part of Jesus' spiritual story about two sons in its chorus: "I once was lost, but now am found..." How was this true of your own life, and how did your experience of the heart of your heavenly Father change you?

Share the Heart of God

• Jesus said that we will witness people streaming from all four corners of the earth in God's kingdom realm. Why is this good news for sharing the heart of God?

• "The Sabbath was made for the sake of people," Jesus revealed in Mark 2:27. Yet we often create rules and barriers around it. How can you and others better share the Sabbath with people to help them experience the heart of God?

- Who in your life is like a lost sheep or coin? How might you join God's mission of rescue to help them be found?

- Luke 15 is filled with stories that help us understand God's heart for the lost. How do you picture heaven's celebration over the lost when they are found?

CONSIDER THIS

God's kingdom realm is the kind of life God always meant for us—in the way we live with him, others, ourselves, and creation. It's also the kind of life we've always longed for. But it's a realm and reign that must be chosen; we need to count the cost of following Jesus into it. Consider what it means to enter God's kingdom realm and what you need to give up to more fully follow Jesus into it.

Lesson 8

Faithfulness and Faith

LUKE 16:1–17:19

*"The one who manages the little he has been given
with faithfulness and integrity will be promoted and trusted
with greater responsibilities. But those who cheat with
the little they have been given will not be considered
trustworthy to receive more."* (Luke 16:10)

To say we're living in an instant-gratification, always-on-the-go, always-connected culture is putting it lightly. This kind of instant living takes a toll on our families, psyche, and finances. It takes a toll on our spiritual lives too. We no longer understand what it means to live a faithful life—to live a "long obedience in the same direction," as one person has put it.

Jesus calls us to such a life. In our reading today we find a spiritual story about a business manager, sharing that people who are faithful in their lives will be trusted with more. In another story, Jesus revealed that how we live in obedience to God's command to love impacts what happens on the other side of death. Jesus invites us to help our fellow Christians maintain this faithfulness. He also commends people who faithfully worship God in response to his help.

While our culture doesn't understand "a long obedience in the same direction," let Jesus' words penetrate your heart and flourish in your soul to help you live faithfully.

Discover the Heart of God

- After reading Luke 16:1–17:19, what did you notice, perhaps for the first time? What questions do you have? What did you learn about the heart of God?

- What one word would you choose to summarize Jesus' teachings in chapter 16?

- How did Jesus explain the spiritual story of the dishonest manager?

- How many times did Jesus say we should forgive others in one day?

- The Samaritan leper in 17:11–19 whom Jesus healed received something extra from him. The other nine Jesus healed did not. What did he receive?

Explore the Heart of God

- How do you think it looks for the sons of light to be as shrewd as the sons of darkness in their interactions with others?

- Why is it impossible for Christians to serve the two "masters," God and wealth?

- What does Jesus' spiritual story about the rich man and Lazarus teach us about death, the afterlife, and judgment?

- Why did Jesus tell us to stay alert to our fellow believer's "condition" (17:2)? What did he mean by this, and how might that look practically?

- According to Jesus, how powerful is the small measure of faith we have in situations, and why does that matter to our everyday lives?

- When we serve people, it's tempting to receive praise for it. How did Jesus say we should respond instead, and how does this deepen our understanding of the heart of God?

Experience the Heart of God

- Jesus said those who faithfully manage what little they have been given will be given more responsibility. But those who cheat with what little they've been given will not be considered trustworthy to receive more. How are you handling what God has entrusted to you?

- Has someone ever been alert to your condition and corrected you for it? How did that feel, and what was the result?

- When Jesus healed ten men, only one returned to give thanks and praise. How should this example convict us when we tangibly experience the heart of God?

Share the Heart of God

- How can you use the wealth of this world to shrewdly share the heart of God with those in your life?

- What does Jesus' spiritual story about the rich man and Lazarus tell us about the urgency of sharing the heart of God with people in our lives?

- In 17:1–10, Jesus tied forgiveness and faith together with simply doing what is expected of us. What does God expect of us when it comes to forgiveness?

- When we are alert to our brother's condition and try to correct him, how is that a way we share the heart of God?

CONSIDER THIS

Jesus invites us to live "a long obedience in the same direction." He invites us to a life of faithfulness. And at the end, after faithfully obeying all that he has commanded, he calls on us to simply say, "We are mere servants, undeserving of special praise, for we are just doing what is expected of us and fulfilling our duties." May we faithfully do what's expected of us as followers of Jesus until the day of his return.

Lesson 9

Let Go of Life to Discover True Life

LUKE 17:20–19:27

"Anyone who leaves his home behind and chooses
God's kingdom realm over wife, children, parents, and family, it
will come back to him many more times in this lifetime,
and in the age to come, he will inherit even more than that—
he will inherit eternal life!" (Luke 18:29–30)

Today's reading could be summarized by two stories about two wealthy men who encountered Jesus.

First, a Jewish nobleman questioned Jesus about gaining eternal life, which was more of a challenge than a genuine interest in deeper revelation. Even though he knew what the man was up to, Jesus answered him: obey the commandments. The Jewish nobleman was pleased because he claimed he'd been doing just that. Jesus knew otherwise, so he told him to sell everything and give his money to the poor. Instead of responding in obedience to Jesus' lordship, the man walked away.

Now compare this response to a Roman tax collector, Zacchaeus. When Jesus arrived into his city, Zacchaeus pulled out all the stops to get a glimpse of him. When he did, Jesus invited himself over to his house, and Zacchaeus received him with joy! He also responded to the lordship of Jesus by giving half of all he owned to the poor and pledging to pay back the people he had cheated.

These two men encountered the same Jesus. Yet they responded very differently. Zacchaeus discovered what you'll discover: it's only when we let go of our life and surrender it to Jesus that we discover true life.

Discover the Heart of God

- After reading Luke 17:20–19:27, what did you notice, perhaps for the first time? What questions do you have? What did you learn about the heart of God?

- Describe how the proud religious leader and despised tax collector in Jesus' parable about prayer approached God. Which one did Jesus say left home right with God?

- What did the disciples do to those who were bringing their children to Jesus for a blessing? How did Jesus respond?

- A wealthy nobleman told Jesus he was obeying all the commandments, yet Jesus said there was still one thing missing in his life. What did he tell him to do?

- Based on 19:11, what expectations did the Jewish people have of Jesus?

Explore the Heart of God

- What do you think it means for the end of the world as we know it that Jesus compares it to the days of Noah and Lot? What does it say about people's need to respond to Jesus now, since he says they "won't have time" at the day of his appearing (17:31)?

- If you ever pray with a child, as Jesus did in 18:15–17, and then pray with an adult, you'll notice the difference. A child almost always has an open heart to everything you pray, but an adult can ignore your words. What does this tell us about how to receive God's kingdom?

- What does it tell us about the wealthy nobleman's spiritual life that he was devastated when Jesus told him to sell everything?

- When the blind man saw Jesus, he identified him as the "Son of David" and "Lord" and then came to him for healing. What does this say about the kind of faith he had in Jesus and the kind of faith Jesus rewarded by giving the man sight and new life?

- Compare the responses of the wealthy nobleman and Zacchaeus to Jesus' invitations to follow. What made Zacchaeus's response so different?

Experience the Heart of God

- If Jesus is right that God's kingdom realm is already expanding in our midst, how does it look to experience his kingdom realm right here and now?

- Jesus taught the disciples to keep praying and never lose hope. How should this encourage us as we seek the heart of God through answered prayer?

- How should Jesus' parable of the religious leader and tax collector influence how we experience the heart of God?

- The issue between the wealthy nobleman and Jesus was one of full devotion. How would you feel if Jesus asked you to give up something completely and forever? What might you need to leave behind to be fully devoted to following Jesus?

- Jesus told Zacchaeus that life had come to him when he aligned his heart with God's and committed to help others instead of oppress them. What changes can you make to grow in life as Zacchaeus did?

Share the Heart of God

- How should Jesus' description of the end compel us to share the heart of God and story of Christ with people we know?

• Why are Jesus' instructions about God's kingdom realm and children good news for those with whom we share the heart of God?

• Jesus said, "What appears humanly impossible is more than possible with God. For God can do what man cannot" (18:27). How should this encourage us as we share the heart of God?

• What does Zacchaeus's reaction tell us about people who see Jesus when we share his true heart with people?

CONSIDER THIS

As Luke depicted Jesus' final approach to Jerusalem, he continued to sharpen Jesus' message. His call became ever clearer to embrace his example and take it as our own, to not live for this life but for the next, to let go of our life in order to find true life. If you have not wholly given yourself to follow after Jesus, take time right now to commit yourself fully to him.

Lesson 10

———

A Week of Warning

LUKE 19:28–21:38

"You will be hated by all because of my life in you.
But don't worry. My grace will never desert you
or depart from your life." (Luke 21:16–18)

Luke has given us a truly magnificent portrait of the life, mission, and ministry of Jesus! We've come a long way in the story of Jesus, and the final week in that story unfolds much in the way it began: with exhortations to faithfulness and calls to follow Jesus. But Jesus' words take a turn.

Jesus has said all he needs to say to the religious and social elite, because he has silenced them completely, having answered their every challenge and scheme to entrap him. So he moves on to warn his followers: everyone who laid down their coats before his donkey and proclaimed him king. His words for these followers include many warnings about persecution, the destruction of Jerusalem, and the climactic events that will precede his second coming.

Amidst Jesus' warnings of disaster, it can be difficult to hear the same heart that healed the sick and raised the dead. Yet it's still there, speaking words of strength, hope, and comfort. As you encounter and explore today's reading, remember the person you've already encountered in

Luke's story. Listen for his voice. Continue to open your heart to him, and you will hear him.

Discover the Heart of God

- After reading Luke 19:28–21:38, what did you notice, perhaps for the first time? What questions do you have? What did you learn about the heart of God?

- How did the high priests, experts in the law, and the leaders of Jerusalem respond to Jesus cleansing the temple?

- In 20:20–26, Luke reported that the Jewish religious leaders sent spies to trap Jesus. How did Jesus respond?

- Some people believe that Jesus never claimed to be the Messiah. How does 20:41–44 answer this claim?

- Jesus didn't sugarcoat any of his warnings in 21:5–19, yet he did offer some words of comfort. What are they?

- Jesus talked about his second coming in 21:27–28. Why did he say we will celebrate on that day of his arrival?

Explore the Heart of God

- Even though Jesus marched toward his death as he entered Jerusalem, he indicated that praise was necessary in that moment. Why was he right—why was praise so important?

- When Jesus answered the Sadducees in 20:34–39, he clearly taught that God raises the dead into eternal life. Why was it so important for Jesus to teach this truth?

- Jesus cautioned his disciples against becoming like the "pretentious experts of the law" (20:46), who had an appearance of godliness but who were actually evil. Looking at 20:45–47, how can you tell the difference between pretend and genuine godliness?

- What does Jesus' teaching about the widow's offering reveal about the heart of God? How should it impact how we talk about giving in the church?

- Jesus prophesied that his followers would experience troubles and persecutions. In 21:10–19, he taught that we should not prepare our defense before we stand on trial, but rather let his wisdom come to us in that moment. What does this show us about his heart to help us during troubled times, especially during times of persecution?

Experience the Heart of God

- Have you received Jesus' entrance into your own life in the same way the crowds received Jesus into their city?

- If it's true that Jesus' authority to teach about salvation is from heaven, what does that mean for you and your experience of the heart of God?

- How might it look in your life to sacrifice out of your own poverty, like the poor widow? What is an amount you can commit to the Lord?

- What is your reaction to what Jesus says will happen to Christians leading to the end of the age? How should 20:18 encourage us?

- Jesus warns us from allowing our hearts to grow cold. How do you think this might happen in the Christian life? How can we "remain passionate" and "keep a constant watch"?

Share the Heart of God

- How might it look in your life to view your city with the same eyes that Jesus had for his city? How might it change how you share the heart of God?

- In answer to the Sadducees, Jesus said that God is "the God who raises the dead" (20:38). Why is this the best news you could give as you share the heart of God with people?

- How should 21:25–28 motivate us to share the heart of God?

- Sometimes, with our focus on evangelism, we forget that we need to share the heart of God with fellow brothers and sisters in Christ. How might it look to help Christians in your life remain passionate and watchful and not grow cold by sharing the heart of God?

CONSIDER THIS

It can be difficult for those of us who have lived far away from life-threatening persecution to identify with what Jesus speaks in some of these passages. Yet his call to give ourselves completely to him is clearer than ever before. Determine today to follow Jesus wherever he may call you, no matter the cost.

Lesson 11

Death of the Innocent One

LUKE 22–23

*"I promise you—this very day
you will enter Paradise with me."* (Luke 23:43)

He was led like a lamb to be slaughtered, Isaiah says. Like a pure, spotless, innocent, silent sheep before his shearers, Jesus was executed like a common criminal on a Roman cross.

Yet he had done no wrong! We were the reason he died; it was our fault he was executed. Isaiah reminds us that we all have blood on our hands:

> It was because of our rebellious deeds that he was pierced and because of our sins that he was crushed. He endured the punishment that made us well and his bruises have brought us healing. Like wandering sheep we have all gone astray. Each of us have left God's paths and chosen our own. And the Lord has laid the guilt of all our sins upon him. (Isaiah 53:5–6)

Jesus was despised and betrayed, led away and beaten after an unjust trial—for you and the world. His body was broken apart, his blood was shed—for you and the world. He humbly submitted to God's punishment for sin—for you and the world.

Jesus, the Innocent One, paid the price in your place—so you can be in relationship with him forever!

Discover the Heart of God

- After reading Luke 22–23, what did you notice, perhaps for the first time? What questions do you have? What did you learn about the heart of God?

- What did Jesus do and say when he sat to eat the Passover meal with his disciples?

- Luke 22:23–24 shows an interesting contrast: At first the disciples wonder who among themselves might be the one to betray Jesus. But then they do something that is completely opposite. What did they do, and how did Jesus respond?

• What did Jesus say to the Jewish religious leaders that served to condemn him in their eyes? To them, why was this statement so grievous?

• After the Roman soldiers beat Jesus, the religious leaders asked him if he was the Messiah. How did Jesus respond?

• How many times was Jesus declared innocent before he was finally crucified?

Explore the Heart of God

• What is Passover, and why is it significant that Jesus died during this celebration? What does Jesus mean that the bread was his "body" and the cup of wine his "blood"?

- Twice in 22:14–18 Jesus spoke of feasting again with his disciples at the banquet of the kingdom of God. What insight does this give us into Jesus' mind-set as he approached the cross?

- What does Jesus' prayer in the garden of Gethsemane reveal about the heart of God?

- As Jesus was nailed to the cross, he prayed a remarkable prayer: "Father, forgive them..." (23:34). As the soldiers stripped him naked and gambled for his clothes, as they piled on the abuse, as they drove nails into his body—he asked his Father to forgive them. Why would Jesus pray such a prayer in that moment?

- What did Jesus say at the end of his crucifixion? What happened?

Experience the Heart of God

- Sometimes the Lord's Supper can feel like just a religious cere-
  mony. But it is rooted in the Passover meal Jesus shared with his
  disciples, when he said the bread represented his body and the cup
  his blood. How should this symbolism deepen your understanding
  of the heart of God?

- Luke 22:23 is one of the most haunting verses in the Bible because
  it indicates the disciples had no idea which of them might betray
  Jesus. None of them expected it! Imagine being one of the disciples
  in that moment. How would you feel? What would you be thinking?

- In Jesus' greatest moment, he spent time praying to his Father and
  then called his disciples to do the same. What does this say to you
  about the power and importance of prayer during our own times
  of need?

- What does it mean to you that Jesus prayed for the "cup of agony" (the cross) to be taken away, and yet he wanted God's will to be done and then went to the cross?

- In light of what Jesus endured on the cross, what is your response to the way Jesus died for your sins?

Share the Heart of God

- Paul said that every time Christians celebrate the Lord's Supper they proclaim the death and resurrection of Jesus. How can this meal be the perfect occasion to share the heart of God?

- Why is the cross truly good news for the people you know who are far from God? How might it look in your life to share this good news with them so they too can share in the heart of God?

- Before Jesus died, another man who was hanging next to Jesus begged Jesus to show him grace and take him into his everlasting kingdom. Jesus promised the repentant criminal that he would be with him in "Paradise." Why is this such good news for those with whom you desire to share the heart of God?

CONSIDER THIS

The message of Jesus on the cross is the most important message that everyone needs to hear. It is a message of forgiveness, a new start, and a new life defined by Jesus' perfect innocence. Embrace afresh today the sacrifice Jesus made for you. Let his innocence fill you with a deeper sense of having been washed clean and set free than you have ever had before.

Lesson 12

Life Wins and Begins

LUKE 24

"Why would you look for the Living One in a tomb?
He is not here, for he has risen!" (Luke 24:5)

In many ways, Luke's story about Jesus ends the way it began. The first several chapters contain numerous angelic encounters bringing almost unbelievable news. Luke's final chapter contains numerous heavenly encounters as well, along with another unexpected news bulletin.

Just as the initial messengers brought news of miraculous natural birth, these latter encounters brought news of miraculous *supernatural* birth—new life for all mankind! The women who came to Jesus' tomb looking for him were consumed with Jesus' death—thinking about it, mourning it, wondering what to do next. But then light pierced their darkness, life flooded the tombs of their hearts and minds, and they could no longer find death within themselves.

Jesus rose from the dead, and so they found new life in him! As they found new life in Jesus, so may we, for this is why Jesus had to suffer and die. He died for us so that we might live for him, set free from all that would oppress our hearts now, and ultimately become free into the perfection of life that awaits us in eternity.

It's an invitation offered to all, a gift given to all those who will simply follow Jesus.

Discover the Heart of God

- After reading Luke 24, what did you notice, perhaps for the first time? What questions do you have? What did you learn about the heart of God?

- What did Miriam Magdalene, Joanna, and Miriam, mother of Jesus, discover when they went to Jesus' tomb? How did they react to their discovery? How did the disciples react to their news?

- What happened to the two disciples on the road to the town of Emmaus? How were they feeling when Jesus approached them on the road?

- What did Jesus do that made the men's hearts burn on the road to Emmaus?

- How did Jesus reassure his disciples when he appeared to them?

- What was Jesus doing when he ascended into heaven?

Explore the Heart of God

- Can you recall any of the instances throughout Jesus' ministry when he told his followers of his resurrection? List them here.

- Imagine being with Peter as he ran to the tomb to see for himself the news of the empty tomb. How would you have felt in that moment? What would you be thinking?

- Jesus' first response to the men on the road seemed harsh, but he didn't stop there. In fact, we get the feeling he met those men for the specific purpose of explaining to them the Scriptures about himself. What does this say about Jesus' heart?

- The disciples were terrified when Jesus appeared among them, but Jesus' first words were words of comfort. In fact, he took several steps to comfort them before he finally told them they would be his witnesses to the nations. How does this help us understand the way God works with us?

- After Jesus was raised from the dead, he showed the disciples the scars on his hands and feet, and then he ate some food. What does this tell us about what our own resurrected bodies will be like at the end when Christ comes to raise us from the dead?

- Jesus gave the disciples a mission but required them to stay until they received his powerful, ever-present help. Why did Jesus give them these instructions?

Experience the Heart of God

- What do you think about the testimony of the women that the tomb was empty and Jesus was alive? What does it tell us about the heart of God that it was indeed empty?

• When the women told the disciples that angels appeared to them saying Jesus was alive, the men doubted them until God opened their hearts to understand. What happened in your life to open your heart so that you could understand God's truth and heart?

• The men in Emmaus realized their hearts felt the same way talking with Jesus on the road as they had when he taught them in his ministry. How do you know when Jesus is talking to you?

• In response to the resurrected Christ, the disciples were "overwhelmed and ecstatic with joy" as they headed back to Jerusalem. They also met every day in the temple, "praising and worshiping God" (24:52–53). How would it look in your own life to respond to the resurrected Christ in this way?

Share the Heart of God

- Why is the resurrection so crucial to our message when we share the heart of God? Why is it truly good news?

- To explain to a few men on their way to Emmaus why he had to suffer and rise to glory, Jesus "carefully unveiled to them the revelation of himself throughout the Scripture" (24:27). How might what Jesus did guide how we share the heart of God too?

- After Jesus opened the men's eyes in Emmaus, they immediately ran seven miles back to Jerusalem to tell the others they had seen Jesus. What would move you to be so passionate to tell your friends about Jesus?

CONSIDER THIS

While the message of Jesus' death is the most important message everyone must hear, it leaves us hopeless without the message of Jesus' resurrection. In Jesus' death we have forgiveness, but in Jesus' life we also have life! Death had no hold on him; neither does it have any hold on those who believe in him. Thank Jesus from the depths of your heart today for the life you have in him!